THE LOONS BOOK

OF 21 POSTCARDS

Salmo trutti

P.O. BOX 280070
SAN FRANCISCO • CALIFORNIA 94128-0070

ISBN: 1-56313-881-6
TITLE #: ST6881

Salmo trutti publishes a large line of photographic books and postcard books. _Please write for more information._

Printed in Korea

LOONS
COMMON LOON PERFORMING WINGFLAP

PUBLISHED BY *Salmo trutti* • SAN FRANCISCO, CALIFORNIA

LOONS

COMMON LOON FAMILY AMONG LILY PADS

PUBLISHED BY *Salmo trutti* • SAN FRANCISCO, CALIFORNIA

LOONS
COMMON LOON

PUBLISHED BY *Salmo trutti* • SAN FRANCISCO, CALIFORNIA

LOONS

YELLOW-BILLED LOON TURNS EGGS IN NEST

PUBLISHED BY *Salmo trutti* • SAN FRANCISCO, CALIFORNIA

LOONS

RED-THROATED LOON ON NEST

PUBLISHED BY *Salmo trutti* • SAN FRANCISCO, CALIFORNIA

LOONS

COMMON LOON WITH SMALL PERCH IN BILL

PUBLISHED BY *Salmo trutti* • SAN FRANCISCO, CALIFORNIA

LOONS
PACIFIC LOONS

PUBLISHED BY *Salmo trutti* • SAN FRANCISCO, CALIFORNIA

LOONS
COMMON LOON WITH CHICK

PUBLISHED BY *Salmo trutti* • SAN FRANCISCO, CALIFORNIA

LOONS
RED-THROATED LOON

PUBLISHED BY *Salmo trutti* • SAN FRANCISCO, CALIFORNIA

LOONS
COMMON LOON

PUBLISHED BY *Salmo trutti* • SAN FRANCISCO, CALIFORNIA

LOONS

COMMON LOONS SWIMMING DURING FIRST LIGHT

PUBLISHED BY _Salmo trutti_ • SAN FRANCISCO, CALIFORNIA

LOONS
COMMON LOON WITH CHICKS

PUBLISHED BY *Salmo trutti* • SAN FRANCISCO, CALIFORNIA

LOONS
COMMON LOON FEEDING CHICK

PUBLISHED BY *Salmo trutti* • SAN FRANCISCO, CALIFORNIA

LOONS

PACIFIC LOON

PUBLISHED BY *Salmo trutti* • SAN FRANCISCO, CALIFORNIA

LOONS

COMMON LOON WITH BIRCH TREE IN DISTANCE

PUBLISHED BY *Salmo trutti* • SAN FRANCISCO, CALIFORNIA

LOONS

RED-THROATED LOON ON NEST

PUBLISHED BY *Salmo trutti* • SAN FRANCISCO, CALIFORNIA

LOONS
COMMON LOONS

PUBLISHED BY *Salmo trutti* • SAN FRANCISCO, CALIFORNIA

LOONS
YELLOW-BILLED LOON

PUBLISHED BY *Salmo trutti* • SAN FRANCISCO, CALIFORNIA

LOONS
COMMON LOONS

PUBLISHED BY *Salmo trutti* • SAN FRANCISCO, CALIFORNIA

LOONS

COMMON LOON

PUBLISHED BY *Salmo trutti* • SAN FRANCISCO, CALIFORNIA

LOONS
COMMON LOON FAMILY SWIMMING DURING SUNRISE

PUBLISHED BY *Salmo trutti* • SAN FRANCISCO, CALIFORNIA